The Three Magicians

There was once a boy called Billy,
who went looking for a magician.

He looked in the hot lands
and he looked in the cold lands.

2

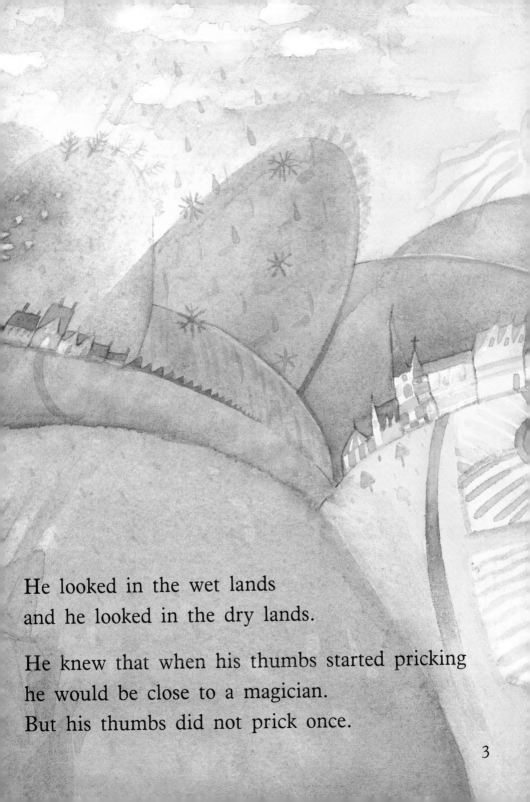

He looked in the wet lands
and he looked in the dry lands.

He knew that when his thumbs started pricking
he would be close to a magician.
But his thumbs did not prick once.

3

At last he came to Blue Land.

He followed a blue road that ran
between blue paddocks, under blue gums,
over blue hills to blue sands by a blue sea.

"There are magicians around," said Billy.
"My thumbs are pricking."

He gathered blue wood and lit a blue fire.
The sparks turned into blue mice
and ran into holes in the sand.

4

After a while a horse came out of the wood.
"What are you looking for, Billy?" it asked.

"I'm looking for a magician," said Billy.

6

"How will you know a magician, Billy?"
asked the horse.

"By his hat," said Billy. "He will wear
a pointed hat, painted with silver stars."

"I am wearing a hat like that," said the horse.

"Yes, but magicians have flowers
in their hair," said Billy.

"I have flowers in my mane," said the horse.

"Yes, but magicians change the world,"
said Billy.

"Look," said the horse, "do you notice
that everything here is blue?
Yet I am all the colors of the world."

"That is true," said Billy,
"but you are still only a horse."

The next day he went on,
still looking for a magician,
and the horse walked along behind him.

After a while Billy came to Red Land.

8

He walked along the red road
under the big redwoods
until he came to red sand by a red sea.

"I know there are magicians around," said Billy.
"My thumbs are pricking more than ever."

9

He gathered red wood and made a red fire.
The sparks turned into red birds
and flew away into the red night.

Out of the shadows came a porcupine.
"What can I do for you, Billy?" it said.

"I'm looking for a magician," Billy replied.

"How will you know a magician, Billy?"

"Well, I will know him by his pointed hat
with golden moons."

"I am wearing a hat like that," said the porcupine.

12

"Yes, but magicians have flowers
in their hair," said Billy.

"Look carefully," said the porcupine.
"I have buttercups and daisies
growing among my quills."

"Yes, I did notice that," said Billy.
"But magicians change the world."

"Do you notice that everything here is red?"
asked the porcupine.
"Yet I am all the colors of the world."

"That's true," said Billy.
"But you're still only a porcupine."

Billy went on the next day
and the horse and the porcupine followed.
After a while he came to Green Land,
and walked along a green road
through the green woods
until he came to green sand by a green sea.

"My thumbs are pricking like pincushions,"
said Billy.
"I know there are magicians around here."

He gathered green wood and lit a green fire.
The sparks turned into green fish
and dived into the sea.

15

Out of the shadows came a girl.
"Hello, Billy," she said.
"Why have you come to Green Land?"

"I'm looking for magicians," he said.

The girl looked at him.
Then she looked at the horse and the porcupine.

"How will you know a magician if you see one?"
she asked him.

"By his hat," said Billy.
"He will wear a pointed hat with black cats on it."

"I am wearing a hat like that," said the girl.

"But magicians have flowers in their hair,"
cried Billy.

"I have flowers in my hair."

"Yes, but magicians change the world."

The girl said, "Do you notice
that everything here is green?
Yet I am walking in the middle of a rainbow?"

16

"Yes, I did notice that," said Billy.
"But you are only a girl."

17

The next morning
Billy said to the girl,
the horse and the porcupine,
"My thumbs are pricking
more and more.
There must be magicians all around me.
They must be too shy to come out
when they see that I have company.
I'd better go on alone."

"Why do you want to find a magician?"
asked the girl.

"Well, I want to be a magician myself some day,"
Billy replied. "I want to change the world."

Then he went off on his own.

The girl, the porcupine and the horse
sat on the edge of the green sea.
The girl played a green violin,
and fish came out of the sea
and danced.

The porcupine
played a red whistle,
and birds came out of the air
and danced.

The horse beat on a blue drum,
and mice came out of the sand and danced.

And as they played
they sang a soft, sad song.

Wander and wonder,
along and around.
Through air, across water,
and over the ground…
Unless you can see
what's in front of your eyes,
You'll never meet magic
or get a surprise.
For all the surprises
will rustle and run,
And magicians live over
the next hill but one.

So Billy went on looking for a magician,
and the three magicians all went home to bed.

24